Dental health cookbook for kids 2024

Fun Recipes for Strong Teeth and Healthy Smiles

Misty j. Font

1

Table of content

CHAPTER 1:
INTRODUCTION

Once upon a time, a young boy named Sam lived in a bustling town surrounded by rolling hills and lush greenery. Sam was known for his bright smile and contagious laughter, but he secretly struggled with dental health.

Sam's journey began when he felt discomfort and pain in his teeth. His once joyful smile had turned into a grimace of discomfort, and he found it difficult to enjoy his favorite foods. Concerned for their son's health, Sam's parents sought advice from their family dentist, who diagnosed him with dental issues caused by poor oral hygiene and unhealthy eating habits.

Sam's parents set out to find solutions to his dental problems and restore his radiant smile. They scoured libraries, consulted dental experts, and searched the internet for resources to help their son with his dental health.

During their search, they discovered a wealth of knowledge - the Dental Health Cookbook for Kids. This cookbook, filled with colorful illustrations and mouthwatering recipes, promised to nourish young bodies while also strengthening teeth and gums. Sam's parents, eager to find a solution, rushed to get the cookbook and begin reading it.

As they flipped through the pages, they were delighted to find a plethora of nutritious and delicious recipes designed specifically for children's dental health. The cookbook promised to help Sam's dental recovery with a variety of culinary delights ranging from crunchy vegetable snacks to calcium-rich smoothies and tooth-friendly desserts.

With their newfound knowledge and inspiration, Sam's parents jumped right into putting the cookbook's recipes to the test. They turned their kitchen into a culinary laboratory, experimenting with colorful fruits, crunchy vegetables, and nutritious ingredients to create meals that would not only satisfy Sam's taste buds but also benefit his dental health.

Sam's palate expanded with each meal prepared using the cookbook's recipes, as did his love for healthy eating. He enjoyed the vibrant flavors of fresh fruits and vegetables, the creamy textures of calcium-rich dairy products, and guilt-free treats that nourished and strengthened his teeth.

Sam's dental health gradually improved as the days passed into weeks and weeks into months. The discomfort and pain that had previously plagued him gradually faded, giving way to a renewed sense of vitality and well-being. His once-dull smile transformed into a radiant beam of joy, illuminating the room wherever he went.

Sam began a transformative journey toward dental recovery with the help of nutritious food and the Dental Health Cookbook for Kids. With each bite of wholesome goodness, he not only nourished his body but also his spirit, embracing a healthy and vital lifestyle that would last his entire life.

So, with his dental health restored and his smile brighter than ever, Sam began a new chapter in his life, one full of confidence, vitality, and the delectable delights of a culinary journey guided by the wisdom of the Dental Health Cookbook for Kids.

Dental health for children

In the hectic world of parenthood, there are numerous priorities competing for our attention. From ensuring our children's quality education to nurturing their emotional well-being, the list seems endless. However, in the midst of this whirlwind, one aspect frequently overlooked but of critical importance: dental health.

It is impossible to overstate the significance of dental health for children. It's not just about having a beautiful smile; it's about laying the groundwork for a lifetime of overall health. Healthy teeth and gums are essential not only for chewing food, but also for speech development and jaw alignment. Furthermore, good oral hygiene habits developed in childhood can significantly lower the risk of dental problems such as cavities, gum disease, and tooth decay later in life.

How Nutrition Affects Dental Health

Nutrition is essential for good dental health. What we eat has a direct impact on the health of our teeth and gum. Sugary snacks and acidic beverages can erode tooth enamel, causing cavities and decay. A balanced diet rich in fruits, vegetables, lean proteins, and dairy products, on the other hand, contains essential nutrients such as calcium, vitamin D, and phosphorus, all of which strengthen teeth and promote gum health.

Recognizing the profound impact of nutrition on dental health, the goal of this cookbook is straightforward: to provide parents and caregivers with the knowledge and tools they need to instill healthy eating habits in their children while prioritizing dental wellness. We hope that by sharing a collection of delicious and nutritious recipes, we can make dental health not only accessible but also enjoyable for children and families.

The following pages contain a treasure trove of mouthwatering dishes that will tantalize your taste buds while strengthening your teeth and gums. From healthy breakfast bites to satisfying dinner delights, each recipe is carefully designed to promote dental health without sacrificing flavor or fun.

CHAPTER 2: UNDERSTAND DENTAL HEALTH

A radiant smile is more than just a symbol of beauty; it reflects a state of overall well-being, including dental health. In this section, we will delve into the complexities of dental wellness, covering the fundamentals of oral hygiene, common dental issues in children, and invaluable tips for maintaining healthy teeth and gums.

Basics of Dental Hygiene

Oral hygiene is the foundation of dental health, consisting of a set of practices designed to maintain the integrity of teeth and gums. The fundamental components of oral hygiene are:

Brushing: Brushing at least twice a day with fluoride toothpaste is essential for removing plaque, which is a sticky film of bacteria that forms on teeth.

Using a soft-bristled toothbrush and gentle, circular motions ensures thorough cleaning while minimizing damage to delicate gum tissue.

Flossing: Flossing helps to clean areas between teeth and along the gumline that a toothbrush cannot reach. Daily flossing removes food particles and plaque, reducing the risk of cavities and gum disease.

Mouthwash: Antimicrobial mouthwashes help to eliminate bacteria and freshen breath. Incorporating mouthwash into your daily oral hygiene routine adds another layer of protection against dental problems.

Healthy Diet: Proper nutrition is essential for oral health. Limiting sugary snacks and acidic beverages lowers the risk of tooth decay, whereas eating calcium-rich foods like dairy products strengthens teeth and bones.

Regular Dental Check-ups: Routine dental visits allow for early detection and treatment of dental problems. Dentists can offer professional cleanings, fluoride treatments, and advice on good oral hygiene.

Common Dental Issues in Children

Despite our best efforts, children may develop a variety of dental problems that require attention. Some of the most common dental problems that children face include:

Cavities, also known as dental caries, occur when acids produced by bacteria erode tooth enamel. Poor oral hygiene, frequent consumption of sugary foods, and insufficient fluoride exposure all contribute to cavity formation.

Gum Disease: Gingivitis is an early stage of gum disease characterized by red, swollen gums that bleed easily. If left untreated, gingivitis can progress to periodontitis, which causes gum recession and tooth loss.

Malocclusion is a misalignment of the teeth or an improper bite that can impair speech, chewing, and facial aesthetics. Common malocclusions include overbite, underbite, and crossbite.

Tooth sensitivity to hot, cold, or sweet stimuli can indicate enamel erosion, gum recession, or tooth decay. Sensitivity can be bothersome and interfere with eating and drinking.

Tips to Maintain Healthy Teeth and Gums

To protect children's dental health, consider the following suggestions:

Begin Early: From infancy, practice oral hygiene by gently cleaning gums with a soft cloth and transitioning to a toothbrush as teeth emerge.

Be a positive role model by brushing and flossing properly and eating a healthy diet rich in fruits, vegetables, and whole grains.

Use Fluoride: Fluoride strengthens tooth enamel and prevents cavities. Ensure that children use fluoride toothpaste and receive professional fluoride treatments as prescribed by their dentist.

Encourage Water Consumption: Water is not only necessary for hydration, but it also helps to rinse away food particles and bacteria, lowering the risk of cavities and increasing saliva production, which neutralizes acids in the mouth.

Brushing: Until children develop the dexterity to brush effectively on their own, supervise their brushing to ensure complete cleaning of all tooth surfaces.

CHAPTER 3: BREAKFAST BITES

Banana and Oat Pancakes

Ingredients:

- one ripe banana.
- 1 egg
- 1/2 cup rolled oats.
- 1/2 teaspoon of cinnamon (optional)

Instructions:

1. Mash the banana in a mixing bowl until smooth.
2. Add the egg and whisk well.
3. Stir in the rolled oats and cinnamon until thoroughly combined.
4. Heat a nonstick skillet over medium heat and add small amounts of the batter.
5. Cook until bubbles appear on the surface, then flip and finish until golden brown
6. Serve warm, with a dollop of Greek yogurt or a drizzle of honey.

Fruit & Yogurt Parfait

Ingredients:

- Greek yogurt
- Mixed berries: strawberries, blueberries, raspberries
- Granola

Instructions:

1. In a glass or bowl, combine Greek yogurt, mixed berries, and granola.

2. Repeat the layers until the container is full.

3. Serve immediately as a healthy, tooth-friendly breakfast option.

Spinach and cheese omelette

Ingredients:

- Two eggs.

- A handful of baby spinach leaves.

- Shredded cheese (e.g., cheddar, mozzarella, or your choice)

- Add salt and pepper to taste.

Instructions:

1. In a mixing bowl, beat together the eggs and season with salt and pepper.

2. Heat a nonstick skillet over medium heat, then add the baby spinach leaves.

3. Once the spinach has wilted, pour the beaten eggs over it.

4. Sprinkle shredded cheese over one half of the omelette.

5. Fold the other half over the cheese, then cook until the cheese melts and the eggs set.

6. Serve hot with whole wheat toast or a side of fruit.

Whole Wheat Banana Muffins

Ingredients:

- 1/2 cups whole wheat flour.
- 1 teaspoon of baking powder.
- 1/2 teaspoon of baking soda.
- 1/4 teaspoon salt.
- 3 ripe, mashed bananas
- 1/4 cup honey or maple syrup.
- 1/4 cup unsweetened applesauce.

- 1/4 cup milk of your choice (dairy or non-dairy).
- 1 egg
- 1 teaspoon of vanilla extract.

Instructions:

1. Preheat the oven to 350°F/175°C and line a muffin tin with paper liners.
2. In a large mixing bowl, combine the mashed bananas, honey, maple syrup, applesauce, milk, egg, and vanilla extract.
3. In a separate bowl, mix together the whole wheat flour, baking powder, baking soda, and salt.
4. Gradually combine the dry and wet ingredients, stirring until just combined.
5. Spoon the batter into the muffin cups, filling them about two-thirds full.

6. Bake for 18 to 20 minutes, or until a toothpick inserted in the center comes out clean.

7. Let the muffins cool before serving.

Apple and Cinnamon Baked Oatmeal Cups

Ingredients:

- 2 cups of rolled oats.
- 1 teaspoon of baking powder.
- 1/2 teaspoon of cinnamon.
- 1/4 teaspoon salt.
- 1 cup milk of your choice (dairy or non-dairy).
- 1/4 cup maple syrup.
- 1 egg
- 1 teaspoon of vanilla extract.
- One apple, grated or finely chopped

Instructions:

1. Preheat the oven to 350°F/175°C and grease a muffin tin with cooking spray.

2. In a large mixing bowl, combine the rolled oats, baking powder, cinnamon, and salt.

3. In a separate bowl, mix together the milk, maple syrup, egg, and vanilla extract.

4. Pour the wet ingredients into the dry ingredients and stir until thoroughly combined.

5. Fold in the grated or chopped apples.

6. Spoon the oatmeal mixture into the muffin cups, filling them about 3/4 full.

7. Bake for 25-30 minutes, or until the tops turn golden brown and set.

8. Let the oatmeal cups cool before removing them from the muffin tin.

Banana Oat Cookies

Ingredients:

- Ripe bananas.

- Rolled oats

- Cinnamon and honey (optional)

Instructions:

1. In a bowl, mash ripe bananas and add rolled oats and cinnamon.

2. If you want it sweeter, add honey.

3. Place spoonfuls of the mixture on a baking sheet.

4. Bake in the oven until the cookies are golden brown. Let cool before serving.

Veggie-Rich Pasta Salad

Ingredients:

- whole wheat pasta.

- Cherry tomatoes

- Cucumber

- Broccoli

- Black olives

- Italian dressing

Instructions:

1. Cook the pasta according to the package directions and let it cool.

2. Chop the cherry tomatoes, cucumbers, broccoli, and black olives.

3. Toss cooked pasta and chopped vegetables with Italian dressing.

4. Serve chilled for a refreshing and nutritious salad.

Strawberry-Banana Frozen yogurt pops

Ingredients:

- Greek Yogurt.
- Strawberries
- Banana and honey (optional)

Instructions:

1. Blend the Greek yogurt, strawberries, banana, and honey until smooth.

2. Pour the mixture into the popsicle molds.

3. Insert the popsicle sticks and freeze until solid.

4. Serve frozen yogurt pops as a refreshing and healthy dessert.

Crunchy Chickpea Snack

Ingredients:

- Canned chickpeas.
- Ingredients: Olive oil, paprika, garlic powder.
- Salt

Instructions:

1. Rinse and drain the chickpeas, then pat them dry with a paper towel.

2. Toss the chickpeas with olive oil, paprika, garlic powder, and salt.

3. Spread the chickpeas on a baking sheet and bake until crisp.

4. Allow to cool before serving as a crunchy and satisfying snack.

CHAPTER 4: LUNCHTIME TREATS

Turkey and Cheese Roll-ups

Ingredients:

- sliced turkey breast.
- Sliced cheese (cheddar, Swiss, or your preference)
- Whole wheat tortillas.
- Leafy greens (lettuce and spinach)

- Mustard or hummus is optional.

Instructions:

1. Spread a whole wheat tortilla with mustard or hummus, as desired.
2. Place sliced turkey breast, cheese, and leafy greens on top.
3. Roll tightly and cut into bite-size pieces.
4. Serve as a protein-rich, tooth-friendly lunch option.

Vegetable and bean quesadillas

Ingredients:

- whole wheat tortillas.
- Mixed vegetables (bell peppers, onions, corn, and spinach).
- Cooked beans (black and kidney beans)
- Shredded cheese (cheddar or Monterey Jack)
- Olive oil

Instructions:

1. In a medium-size skillet, heat the olive oil.

2. Add the mixed vegetables and cooked beans to the skillet and cook until tender.

3. Place a whole wheat tortilla in the skillet and top with shredded cheese.

4. Spread the vegetable and bean mixture over half of the tortilla.

5. Fold the other half over the filling, pressing down gently.

6. Cook until the cheese melts and the tortilla turns golden brown on both sides.

7. Cut into wedges and serve with salsa or Greek yogurt to dip.

Pita Pocket Sandwiches

Ingredients:

- whole wheat pita pockets.
- Grilled chicken strips or falafel
- Chopped tomatoes

- Shredded lettuce

- Sliced cucumbers

- Greek yogurt or Tahini sauce

Instructions:

1. Cut whole wheat pita pockets in half to make pockets.

2. Fill each pocket with grilled chicken strips or falafel balls, chopped tomatoes, shredded lettuce, and thinly sliced cucumbers.

3. Drizzle with Greek yogurt or tahini sauce to add flavor.

4. Serve as a healthy and filling lunch option.

Vegetable and Rice Stir-Fry

Ingredients:

- Cooked brown rice.

- Mixed vegetables (bell peppers, broccoli, carrots, and snap peas).

- Firm tofu or cooked shrimp.

- Soy sauce

- Garlic

- Ginger

- Olive oil

Instructions:

- In a medium-size skillet, heat the olive oil.

- Stir in the minced garlic and ginger, then the mixed vegetables and tofu or cooked shrimp.

- Stir-fry until the vegetables are tender and crisp, and the tofu or shrimp is thoroughly heated.

- Pour cooked brown rice into the skillet and drizzle with soy sauce.

- Cook, stirring frequently, until everything is fully combined and heated through.

- Serve hot for a flavorful, tooth-friendly lunch.

Rainbow Vegetable Wraps

Ingredients:

- whole wheat tortillas.
- Hummus
- Sliced bell peppers (red, yellow, and green)
- Shredded carrots
- Sliced cucumbers
- Avocado slices
- Baby spinach leaves.

Instructions:

1. Spread the hummus evenly on each whole wheat tortilla.
2. Add sliced bell peppers, shredded carrots, sliced cucumbers, avocado slices, and baby spinach leaves on top.
3. Roll up tightly and cut in half.
4. Serve as a colorful and nutritionally dense lunch option.

Chicken and vegetable skewers

Ingredients:

- Cubed chicken breasts.
- Bell peppers cut into chunks.
- Cherry tomatoes
- zucchini, sliced
- Red onion, chopped into chunks
- Ingredients include olive oil and garlic powder.
- Paprika
- Salt and pepper.

Instructions:

1. Preheat the grill to medium-high heat.
2. Thread chicken cubes and various vegetables onto skewers.
3. Drizzle olive oil and season with garlic powder, paprika, salt, and pepper.

4. Grill the skewers for 8-10 minutes, turning occasionally, until the chicken is fully cooked and the vegetables are tender.

5. Serve hot as a protein-packed, tooth-friendly lunch option.

Tuna Salad Lettuce Wraps

Ingredients:

- canned tuna.
- Greek yogurt or mayonnaise.
- Dijon mustard
- Chopped celery
- Chopped red onions
- Salt and pepper.
- lettuce leaves

Instructions:

1. In a bowl, combine canned tuna, Greek yogurt or mayonnaise, Dijon mustard, chopped celery, and chopped red onion.

2. Season with salt and pepper to taste.

3. Spoon the tuna salad onto the lettuce leaves.

4. Roll up and serve for a refreshing and protein-rich lunch.

Cheesy vegetable quesadillas

Ingredients:

- whole wheat tortillas.
- Shredded cheese (cheddar or Monterey Jack)
- Mixed vegetables (bell peppers, onions, corn, and spinach).
- Olive oil

Instructions:

1. In a medium-size skillet, heat the olive oil.

2. Place a whole wheat tortilla in the skillet and top with shredded cheese.

3. Layer mixed vegetables on half of the tortilla.

4. Fold the other half over the filling, pressing down gently.

5. Cook until the cheese melts and the tortilla turns golden brown on both sides.

6. Cut into wedges and serve with salsa or Greek yogurt to dip.

Pasta Salad With Chicken And Vegetables

Ingredients:

- whole wheat pasta.

- Grilled chicken breast, diced

- Mixed vegetables (bell peppers, cherry tomatoes, and cucumbers).

- Olive oil

- Lemon juice

- Fresh herbs (parsley and basil)

- Salt and pepper.

Instructions:

1. Cook whole wheat pasta according to package directions and allow it to cool.

2. In a large mixing bowl, combine the cooked pasta, diced grilled chicken breast, mixed vegetables, and fresh herbs.

3. Drizzle with olive oil and lemon juice.

4. Season with salt and pepper to taste.

5. Toss to combine, then serve as a colorful and nutritious lunch option.

CHAPTER 5: DINNER DELIGHTS

Baked Lemon-Herb Salmon

Ingredients:

- salmon fillets.
- Lemon
- Fresh herbs (like dill and parsley)
- Olive oil
- Salt and pepper.

Instructions:

1. Preheat the oven to 375° Fahrenheit (190° Celsius).

2. Place the salmon fillets on a parchment-lined baking sheet.

3. Drizzle olive oil and squeeze fresh lemon juice over the salmon.

4. Season with salt, pepper, and freshly chopped herbs.

5. Bake for 12-15 minutes, or until the salmon flakes easily with a fork.

6. Serve with steamed vegetables and whole grain rice for a healthy dinner.

Chicken and Vegetable Stir-Fry

Ingredients:

- Sliced chicken breast.

- Mixed vegetables (bell peppers, broccoli, carrots, and snap peas).

- Garlic

- Ginger

- Soy sauce

- Olive oil

- Cooked brown rice.

Instructions:

1. Heat the olive oil in a wok or large skillet over medium-high heat.

2. Cook the sliced chicken breast until browned and cooked through.

3. Remove the chicken from the skillet and set it aside.

4. In the same skillet, if necessary, add a little more olive oil, then the minced garlic and ginger.

5. Stir in the mixed vegetables and cook until tender-crisp.

6. Return the cooked chicken to the skillet, and drizzle with soy sauce.

7. Cook for another 2-3 minutes, stirring continuously.

8. Serve hot with cooked brown rice for a flavorful and tooth-friendly meal.

Vegetable and Lentil Soup

Ingredients:

- Lentils.
- Mixed vegetables (carrots, celery, onion, and spinach).
- Vegetable broth
- Garlic
- *Herbs:*
- thyme,
- rosemary,
- bay leaf
- Olive oil
- Salt and pepper.

Instructions:

1. In a large pot, heat the olive oil over medium heat.

2. Sauté minced garlic and diced onion until translucent.

3. Stir in the chopped mixed vegetables and cook until tender.

4. Combine lentils, vegetable broth, and herbs.

5. Bring to a boil, then reduce the heat and simmer until the lentils are tender.

6. Season with salt and pepper to taste.

7. Serve hot for a satisfying and nutritious dinner option.

Turkey and vegetable meatballs

Ingredients:

- Ground turkey.
- Mixed vegetables (bell peppers, zucchini, carrots), grated or finely chopped.
- Whole wheat breadcrumbs
- Egg Garlic powder

- Italian seasoning.
- Salt and pepper.
- Olive oil

Instructions:

1. Preheat the oven to 375°F (190°C), then line a baking sheet with parchment paper.
2. In a large mixing bowl, combine the ground turkey, mixed vegetables, whole wheat breadcrumbs, egg, garlic powder, Italian seasoning, salt, and pepper.
3. Mix until well combined, then shape into meatballs.
4. Place the meatballs on the prepared baking sheet and drizzle with olive oil.
5. Bake the meatballs for 20-25 minutes, or until thoroughly cooked and browned.
6. Serve with marinara sauce and whole wheat pasta or quinoa for a healthy dinner.

Vegetable and Chicken Skewers

Ingredients:

- Chicken breast cut into cubes.
- Mixed vegetables (bell peppers, cherry tomatoes, and zucchini).
- olive oil and garlic powder.
- Paprika
- Salt and pepper.

Instructions:

1. Preheat the grill to medium-high heat.
2. Thread chicken cubes and various vegetables onto skewers.
3. Drizzle olive oil and season with garlic powder, paprika, salt, and pepper.
4. Grill the skewers for 8-10 minutes, turning occasionally, until the chicken is fully cooked and the vegetables are tender.

5. Serve hot with quinoa or brown rice for a protein-rich, tooth-friendly dinner.

Vegetables and Chickpea Curry

Ingredients:

- Cooked chickpeas.
- Mixed vegetables (bell peppers, cauliflower, peas, and carrots).
- Coconut milk
- Curry Paste or Powder
- Garlic
- Ginger
- Olive oil
- Fresh cilantro (optional).
- Cooked brown rice or quinoa

Instructions:

1. In a large skillet, heat olive oil over medium heat.
2. Sauté minced garlic and ginger until fragrant.

3. Stir in the mixed vegetables and cooked chickpeas.

4. Stir in the coconut milk and curry paste or powder until evenly combined.

5. Simmer for 10-15 minutes, until the vegetables are tender.

6. Serve hot with cooked brown rice or quinoa.

7. Garnish with fresh cilantro if desired.

Tomato and basil pasta

Ingredients:

- whole wheat pasta.
- Cherry tomatoes halved
- Garlic
- Olive oil
- Fresh basil leaves.
- Salt and pepper.
- grated Parmesan cheese (optional)

Instructions:

1. Cook whole wheat pasta according to the package instructions.
2. In a skillet, heat the olive oil over medium heat.
3. Add the minced garlic and cook until fragrant.
4. Cook cherry tomatoes in a skillet until softened.
5. Combine cooked pasta, tomato mixture, and torn fresh basil leaves.
6. Season with salt and pepper to taste.
7. If desired, serve hot with grated Parmesan cheese.

Mushroom and spinach risotto

Ingredients:

- Arborio Rice
- mushrooms, sliced
- Baby spinach leaves.
- Vegetable broth Onion

- Garlic

- White wine (optional).

- Olive oil

- Parmesan cheese is optional.

Instructions:

1. In a large pot, heat the olive oil over medium heat.

2. Sauté diced onion and minced garlic until translucent.

3. Stir in the Arborio rice and cook for 1-2 minutes.

4. Add the sliced mushrooms and cook until they release their juices.

5. If using, deglaze the pot with white wine.

6. Gradually add vegetable broth, stirring frequently, until the rice is tender and creamy.

7. Stir in the baby spinach leaves until wilted.

8. If desired, serve hot with grated Parmesan cheese.

Vegetable and Tofu Stir-Fry

Ingredients:

- Cubed firm tofu.
- Mixed vegetables (bell peppers, broccoli, snap peas, and carrots).
- Soy sauce
- Garlic
- Ginger
- Olive oil
- Cooked brown rice.

Instructions:

1. In a medium-size skillet, heat the olive oil.
2. Add the cubed tofu and cook until golden brown on all sides.
3. Remove the tofu from the skillet and set aside.

4. In the same skillet, combine the minced garlic and ginger, then stir in the mixed vegetables.

5. Cook until vegetables are tender and crisp.

6. Return cooked tofu to the skillet and drizzle with soy sauce.

7. Cook for another 2-3 minutes, stirring continuously.

8. Serve hot with cooked brown rice for a protein-packed, tooth-friendly dinner.

Baked Chicken with Vegetable Casserole

Ingredients:

- Chicken thighs or breasts.
- Mixed vegetables (bell peppers, broccoli, carrots, and cauliflower).
- Olive oil
- Garlic powder

- Paprika
- Salt and pepper.

Instructions:

1. Preheat the oven to 375°F (190°C). Grease a baking dish with olive oil.
2. Season chicken thighs and breasts with garlic powder, paprika, salt, and pepper.
3. Place the chicken and mixed vegetables in the prepared baking dish.
4. Drizzle with olive oil and toss to coat.
5. Bake for 25-30 minutes, or until the chicken and vegetables are tender.
6. Serve hot for a healthy and nutritious dinner option.

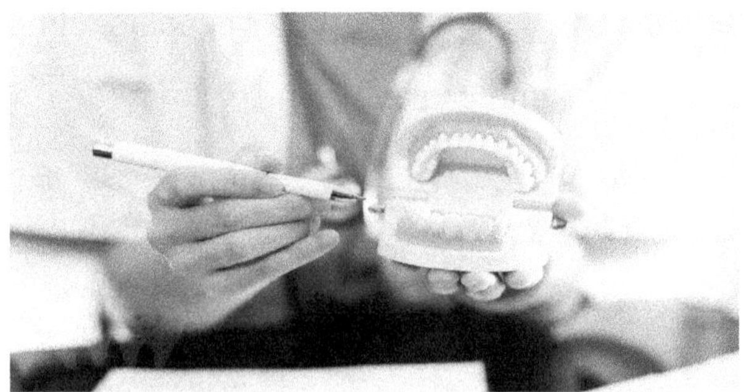

CHAPTER 6: SNACK ATTACKS

Apple Slices and Peanut Butter

Ingredients:

- apples.
- Peanut butter (or almond butter for a nut-free alternative)

Instructions:

1. Wash and slice the apples into wedges.

2. Spread peanut butter over one side of each apple slice.

3. Place on a plate and serve as a crunchy, satisfying snack.

Yogurt Parfait With Berries

Ingredients:

- Greek Yogurt.
- Mixed berries: strawberries, blueberries, raspberries
- Granola (Optional)

Instructions:

1. In a glass or bowl, combine Greek yogurt, mixed berries, and granola.

2. Repeat the layers until the container is full.

3. Serve immediately as a healthy, tooth-friendly snack.

Carrot Sticks and Hummus

Ingredients:

- Carrots.

- Hummus

Instructions:

- Wash and peel carrots, then cut into sticks.

- Serve with hummus to dip.

- Enjoy this crunchy, flavorful snack.

Cheese and Wholegrain Crackers

Ingredients include:

- cheese slices or cubes.

- Wholegrain crackers

Instructions:

1. Place cheese slices or cubes on a plate.

2. Serve with whole-grain crackers for a protein-packed and satisfying snack.

Frozen banana bites

Ingredients:

- Bananas.

- Greek yogurt

- Honey

- Optional toppings include shredded coconut, chopped nuts, and miniature chocolate chips.

Instructions:

1. Slice the bananas into rounds.

2. Spread a thin layer of Greek yogurt across one side of each banana slice.

3. Drizzle with honey and add optional toppings.

4. Place the banana bites on a parchment-lined baking sheet and freeze until firm.

5. Serve as a cool and nutritious frozen treat.

Cucumber and Cream Cheese Roll-ups

Ingredients:

- Cucumber.

- For a lighter option, use Greek yogurt cream cheese.

- Optional fillings include smoked salmon, turkey slices, and avocado.

Instructions:

1. Wash the cucumber and use a vegetable peeler to slice it lengthwise into thin strips.

2. Spread cream cheese over one side of each cucumber strip.

3. If desired, add optional fillings and roll tightly.

4. Secure with a toothpick and serve as a refreshing, crunchy snack.

Popcorn With Parmesan Cheese

Ingredients:

Popcorn Kernels

- Olive oil and grated Parmesan cheese.
- Salt

Instructions:

1. Air-pop popcorn kernels per the manufacturer's instructions.
2. Drizzle with olive oil and toss to coat.
3. Sprinkle with grated Parmesan and a pinch of salt.
4. Serve immediately as a savory, tooth-friendly snack.

Frozen Yogurt Bark

Ingredients:

- Greek Yogurt.
- Honey

- Fresh fruits (berries, sliced bananas, and kiwi)
- Optional toppings include shredded coconut, chopped nuts, and miniature chocolate chips.

Instructions:

1. Line a baking sheet with parchment paper.
2. Combine Greek yogurt and honey, then spread evenly on the prepared baking sheet.
3. Place fresh fruit and optional toppings on top of the yogurt.
4. Freeze until solid, then break into pieces.
5. Serve cold for a refreshing and nutritious snack.

Celery Ants On A Log

Ingredients:

- celery sticks.
- Peanut butter (or almond butter for a nut-free alternative)

- Raisins

Instructions:

1. Wash and trim the celery sticks.
2. Spread peanut butter onto the inside of each celery stick.
3. Press the raisins into the peanut butter.
4. Serve as a fun, crunchy snack that children will enjoy.

Trail mix

Ingredients:

- Various nuts (almonds, cashews, walnuts)
- Dried fruit: raisins, cranberries, and apricots
- Pumpkin seeds.
- Dark chocolate chips are optional.

Instructions:

1. In a mixing bowl, combine assorted nuts, dried fruit, pumpkin seeds, and dark chocolate chips.

2. Portion into individual snack bags for an easy, tooth-friendly snack on the go.

CHAPTER 7: DESSERT RECIPES THAT ARE KIND TO TEETH

Frozen yogurt and berry popsicles

Ingredients:

- Greek Yogurt.

Mixed berries:

- strawberries, blueberries, raspberries
- Honey or maple syrup is optional.

Instructions:

1. Blend Greek yogurt and honey or maple syrup until smooth.

2. Stir in the mixed berries.

3. Pour the mixture into the popsicle molds.

4. Insert the popsicle sticks and freeze until solid.

5. Enjoy these refreshing, tooth-friendly treats!

Banana Oat Cookies

Ingredients:

- Ripe bananas.

- Rolled oats

- Cinnamon (Optional)

- Dark chocolate chips are optional.

Instructions:

1. In a mixing bowl, combine ripe bananas and mash until smooth.

2. Stir in the rolled oats and cinnamon.

3. Optionally, add dark chocolate chips.

4. Place spoonfuls of the mixture on a baking sheet.

5. Bake at 350°F/175°C for 15-20 minutes, or until golden brown.

6. Allow to cool before serving these naturally sweetened cookies.

Baked apples with cinnamon

Ingredients:

1. apples.

2. Cinnamon and honey (optional)

3. Instructions:

4. Core the apples and put them in a baking dish.

5. Sprinkle with cinnamon, and drizzle with honey if desired.

6. Bake at 375°F (190°C) for 25-30 minutes, until tender.

7. Serve warm for a satisfying and tooth-friendly dessert.

Frozen banana "Nice Cream"

Ingredients:

- Bananas.
- Vanilla extract.
- Almond milk (or any milk of your choice).

Instructions:

1. Slice the bananas and freeze until firm.
2. Blend frozen banana slices, almond milk, and vanilla extract until smooth and creamy.
3. Transfer to a bowl and freeze for another 30 minutes.
4. Serve scoops of banana "nice cream" topped with fresh fruit or nuts.

Yogurt and fruit parfait

Ingredients:

- Greek Yogurt.
- Mixed fruit (strawberries, blueberries, and kiwi
- Granola

Instructions:

1. In a glass or bowl, combine Greek yogurt, mixed fruit, and granola.
2. Repeat the layers until the container is full.
3. Serve immediately for a healthy and tooth-friendly dessert option.

Coconut Date Bites

Ingredients:

- Pitted dates.
- Shredded Coconut
- Almonds

Instructions for Vanilla Extract:

1. In a food processor, combine dates, shredded coconut, almonds, and vanilla extract until a sticky dough forms.

2. Roll the mixture into small balls.

3. To coat the balls, roll them in more shredded coconut.

4. Refrigerate for at least 30 minutes before serving these naturally sweet treats.

Chia Seed Pudding

Ingredients:

- chia seeds.
- Milk of your choice (dairy or nondairy)
- Vanilla extract.
- Maple syrup or honey is optional.

Instructions:

1. In a mixing bowl, combine the chia seeds, milk, vanilla extract, and sweetener of choice.

2. Stir well, then set aside for 5 minutes.

3. Stir again to break up any clumps, then cover and chill overnight or at least 4 hours.

4. Serve chilled, garnished with fresh fruit or cinnamon.

Fruit Salad with Honey Lime Dressing

Ingredients:

- Assorted fruit (berries, grapes, melon, and pineapple).
- Honey Lime juice
- Fresh mint leaves (optional).

Instructions:

1. Cut the assorted fruit into bite-sized pieces and place in a bowl.

2. In a separate bowl, combine the honey and lime juice to make the dressing.

3. Toss the fruit in the dressing until well coated.

4. Garnish with fresh mint leaves if desired.

5. Serve immediately for a refreshing and tooth-friendly dessert.

Baked pear crisp

Ingredients:

- Pears.
- Oats
- Almond flour
- Coconut oil
- Maple syrup
- Cinnamon

Instructions:

1. Slice the pears and arrange in a baking dish.

2. To make the crisp topping, combine oats, almond flour, melted coconut oil, maple syrup, and cinnamon.

3. Spread the topping on the pears.

4. Bake at 350°F/175°C for 25-30 minutes, or until the topping is golden brown and the pears are tender.

5. Serve warm with a dollop of Greek yogurt for a healthy dessert.

Chocolate avocado mousse

Ingredients:

- Ripe avocados
- Cocoa powder
- Honey or maple syrup?

Instructions for Vanilla Extract:

1. In a food processor, combine ripe avocados, cocoa powder, honey or maple syrup, and vanilla extract. Process until smooth and creamy.

2. Place in the fridge for at least 30 minutes before serving.

3. Garnish with fresh berries or a sprinkle of cocoa powder.

CHAPTER 8: BEVERAGES FOR BETTER DENTAL HEALTH

Fruit-Infused Water

Ingredients:

- Fresh fruits (strawberries, oranges, lemons, cucumbers).

Water instructions:

1. Slice the fruits into thin rounds or chunks.

2. Place the fruit slices in a pitcher of water.

3. Refrigerate for at least an hour to allow the flavors to combine.

4. Serve chilled for a refreshing and hydrating beverage with no added sugars.

Homemade Fruit Smoothie

Ingredients include :

- mixed berries (strawberries, blueberries, raspberries).
- Banana
- Greek yogurt
- Milk (dairy or nondairy)
- Honey or maple syrup is optional.

Instructions:

1. Blend the mixed berries, banana, Greek yogurt, and milk until smooth.

2. If you want to sweeten it, use honey or maple syrup.

3. Pour into glasses and serve immediately as a nutrient-dense, tooth-friendly beverage.

Green Monster Smoothie

Ingredients:

- Spinach leaves
- Banana
- Pineapple chunks
- Greek yogurt
- Coconut water.

Instructions:

1. Blend the spinach leaves, banana, pineapple chunks, Greek yogurt, and coconut water until smooth.
2. If desired, adjust the sweetness with honey or maple syrup.
3. Serve cold as a green, nutrient-dense beverage.

Watermelon Slushie

Ingredients:

- Watermelon chunks
- Ice cubes
- Lime juice
- Mint leaves (optional).

Instructions:

1. Blend the watermelon chunks, ice cubes, and lime juice until smooth.
2. For an extra burst of flavor, garnish with mint leaves.
3. Serve immediately as a refreshing and hydrating treat ideal for hot days.

Iced herbal tea

Ingredients:

- Herbal tea bags, including chamomile, peppermint, and fruit blends.

- Water

- Honey (Optional)

Instructions:

1. Steep herbal tea bags in hot water according to the package instructions.
2. Allow the tea to cool to room temperature before chilling until cold.
3. If desired, add honey for sweetness.
4. Serve over ice for a soothing, caffeine-free beverage.

Coconut Water and Lime

Ingredients:

- Coconut water.
- Lime juice
- Ice cubes

Instructions:

1. Mix coconut water and lime juice.

2. Add ice cubes and chill.

3. Stir thoroughly and serve immediately as a hydrating, electrolyte-rich beverage.

Berry Blast Smoothie

Ingredients include :

- mixed berries (strawberries, blueberries, raspberries).
- Greek yogurt
- Milk (dairy or nondairy)
- Spinach leaves (optional).
- Honey or maple syrup is optional.

Instructions:

1. Blend the mixed berries, Greek yogurt, milk, and (if using) spinach leaves until smooth.

2. If desired, sweeten with honey or maple syrup.

3. Pour into glasses and serve chilled for a tasty and nutritious beverage.

Homemade lemonade

Ingredients:

- Fresh lemon juice.
- Water
- Honey or maple syrup?
- Ice cubes

Instructions:

1. Combine fresh lemon juice and water in a pitcher.
2. Add honey or maple syrup to taste.
3. Add ice cubes and chill.
4. Stir well and serve as a classic, refreshing beverage with no added sugars.

Minty Cucumber Cooler

Ingredients:

- Cucumber slices
- Mint Leaves

- Lemon slices

- Water

- Ice cubes

Instructions:

- Put cucumber slices, mint leaves, and lemon slices in a pitcher of water.

- Refrigerate for at least an hour to allow the flavors to combine.

- Serve over ice for a refreshing and invigorating beverage.

Orange Creamsicle Smoothie

Ingredients:

- Oranges, peeled and segmented.

- Greek yogurt

- Milk (dairy or nondairy)

- Vanilla extract.

- Honey or maple syrup is optional.

Instructions:

1. Blend together orange segments, Greek yogurt, milk, vanilla extract, and sweetener (if using) until smooth.

2. Adjust the sweetness to your preference.

3. Pour into glasses and serve chilled for a creamy, vitamin C-rich treat reminiscent of a creamsicle.

CHAPTER 9 : BONUS 7-DAY MEAL PLAN

A well-balanced diet is essential for maintaining children's dental health. Parents can help their children's oral hygiene and promote healthy teeth and gums by planning nutritious, low-sugar meals. This 7-day meal plan includes a variety of delicious and nutritious options designed to prioritize dental health while also ensuring that children eat tasty and satisfying meals throughout the week. Let us dive into a week of dental-friendly eating!

Day 1:

Breakfast: Greek yogurt parfait with mixed berries and granola.

Lunch: a turkey and cheese whole wheat wrap with carrot sticks and hummus.

Dinner is baked salmon, roasted sweet potatoes, and steamed broccoli.

Breakfast: Oatmeal topped with sliced bananas and honey.

Lunch: Vegetable-rich lentil soup with whole grain bread.

Dinner: Grilled chicken breast, quinoa, and sautéed spinach.

Breakfast: Whole grain pancakes topped with fresh strawberries and Greek yogurt.

Lunch: Hummus and veggie sandwich on whole wheat bread, with cucumber slices.

Dinner: Vegetable stir-fry with tofu and brown rice.

Breakfast: A smoothie bowl with mango, pineapple, and spinach, topped with granola.

Lunch: Quinoa salad topped with mixed greens, cherry tomatoes, avocado, and grilled chicken.

Dinner: Baked cod, roasted Brussels sprouts, and wild rice.

Day 5:

Breakfast: Scrambled eggs with spinach and feta cheese, served on whole grain toast.

Lunch: Chicken and vegetable skewers served with tzatziki sauce and whole wheat pita bread.

Dinner is turkey meatballs with marinara sauce served over whole wheat pasta.

Day 6:

Breakfast is banana walnut muffins with whole wheat flour and honey.

Lunch: A vegetable-packed pasta salad with cherry tomatoes, cucumbers, black olives, and grilled shrimp.

Dinner: Baked chicken thighs with roasted root vegetables and couscous.

Day 7:

Breakfast: overnight oats with berries, chia seeds, and a splash of almond milk.

Lunch: A turkey and avocado wrap with baby carrots and hummus.

Dinner: Vegetarian chili with cornbread muffins.

CHAPTER 10: CREATIVE WAYS TO INCORPORATE FRUITS AND VEGETABLES INTO KIDS' DIETS

In a world full of processed snacks and sugary treats, it can be difficult for parents to get their children to eat fruits and vegetables. However, incorporating these healthy foods into children's diets does not have to be difficult. With a little imagination and some fun ideas, you can transform fruits and vegetables into exciting and delicious options that children will enjoy. Let's look at some creative ways to make healthy eating fun for kids while also improving their overall well-being.

Create a rainbow plate to encourage kids to eat diverse fruits and vegetables. Arrange colorful fruits and vegetables, such as strawberries, oranges, bananas, kiwi, blueberries, carrots, bell peppers, cucumbers, and purple cabbage, on a plate in rainbow order. Not only does this make mealtime more visually appealing, but it also contains a variety of nutrients.

Veggie Art: Make mealtime an artistic experience by allowing kids to create fun and whimsical designs with fruits and vegetables. Serve a variety of colorful produce alongside whole grain bread, cheese, and spreads such as hummus or cream cheese. Allow them to use their imagination to design faces, animals, or landscapes on their plate. This not only makes eating more enjoyable, but also fosters creativity and exploration.

For a fun snack, thread fruits and vegetables onto skewers. Use bamboo skewers to make colorful and tasty combinations like strawberry-banana, grape-tomato-mozzarella, and pineapple-bell pepper.

These skewers are not only enjoyable to make, but they also make eating fruits and vegetables feel like a special occasion.

Set up a smoothie station with fruits, vegetables, yogurt, and juice to encourage kids to create their own smoothies. Allow them to select their favorite ingredients and blend them together to create delicious and nutritious concoctions. You can even give their smoothies fun names like "Tropical Twist" or "Berry Blast" to make them feel like smoothie experts.

Instead of store-bought chips, encourage kids to snack on homemade veggie chips with a tasty dip. Thinly slice vegetables such as sweet potatoes, zucchini, and beets, toss with olive oil and seasoning, and bake until crisp. Serve with a creamy Greek yogurt and herb dip or hummus for a crunchy and satisfying snack.

Garden Adventure: Take kids to a local farmer's market or grocery store to select their favorite fruits and vegetables. Encourage them to experiment with new or unusual fruits and vegetables to spice up their meals. When they get home, have them help you wash, peel, and chop the produce to make them feel like they're part of the meal preparation process.

Homemade fruit and vegetable popsicles are a refreshing way to beat the summer heat. Blend strawberries, mangoes, spinach, and carrots with a little water or juice before pouring into popsicle molds and freezing until solid. These refreshing treats are ideal for hot summer days and offer a sneaky way to get kids to eat their greens.

Veggie Pasta: Incorporate pureed or finely chopped vegetables into your child's favorite pasta sauce. Carrots, bell peppers, zucchini, and spinach are all easily hidden in tomato sauce or pesto. Serve the veggie-packed pasta with whole wheat noodles for a nutritious and filling meal that kids will never realize is healthy.

For a fun and interactive snack, thread bite-sized fruit onto skewers and serve with creamy yogurt dip. Children can dip their fruit kabobs in the yogurt dip for a tasty and nutritious snack. For an endless variety of flavor combinations, try strawberries and pineapple or grapes and melon.

Veggie Pizza Party: Make pizza night a healthy and interactive experience by allowing kids to top whole wheat pizza crust with their preferred vegetables. Set out a variety of toppings, such as bell peppers, mushrooms, tomatoes, olives, and spinach, and allow them to get creative with their pizzas. Bake until golden and bubbly for a vegetable-packed meal that's sure to be popular.

CHAPTER 11: IDEAS AND TIPS FOR GETTING CHILDREN INVOLVED IN THE KITCHEN

Cooking with children can be an enjoyable and educational experience for both children and adults. It not only teaches important life skills, but it also encourages creativity, confidence, and a passion for healthy eating. However, getting children to help in the kitchen can be difficult at times. With the right ideas and tips, cooking with kids can be a fun and enjoyable activity for the entire family. Let's look at some unique ways to get kids excited about cooking and baking while making lasting memories together.

Begin Simple:

Begin with age-appropriate tasks that the children can easily complete. Younger children can help wash fruits and vegetables, tear lettuce for salads, and mix ingredients in a bowl. As their confidence and skills grow, gradually introduce more complex tasks like measuring ingredients, cutting soft foods with a plastic knife, and assembling sandwiches.

Choose kid-friendly recipes that are simple, nutritious, and appealing to their tastes. Consider dishes like homemade pizzas, fruit smoothies, pasta salads, or mini sandwiches that children can top with their favorite toppings. Consider using colorful ingredients and fun shapes to make cooking more interesting and exciting for children.

Designate a safe and accessible area in the kitchen for children to cook comfortably. Set up a sturdy step stool or platform to allow them to reach countertops and cooking surfaces. Keep kid-friendly utensils, mixing bowls, and aprons within reach to promote independence and reduce frustration.

Encourage children to experiment with different flavors, textures, and ingredients when cooking. Allow them to taste, smell, and touch ingredients in order to stimulate their senses and develop an appreciation for food. Allow them to make decisions and express their creativity by providing options and allowing them to customize their dishes.

Make meal preparation fun for kids by transforming mundane tasks into games. Challenge them to a race to see who can peel carrots and crack eggs faster. Play "I Spy" to help them identify ingredients and kitchen tools. Use counting, sorting, and measuring activities to reinforce math skills while cooking.

To promote safety in the kitchen, teach children basic rules and practices. Show them how to safely use knives, hot surfaces, and kitchen appliances. When using sharp objects or cooking over heat, exercise extreme caution and emphasize the importance of washing hands before and after handling food.

To make cleanup fun, involve children in tidying up the kitchen after cooking. Assign age-appropriate tasks, such as wiping down countertops, washing dishes, and sweeping the floor. Play upbeat music or set a timer to make cleanup feel like a game or a competition.

Recognize and celebrate children's achievements in the kitchen, no matter how small. Show your gratitude for their contributions and creations by displaying or sharing their finished dishes with family and friends. Use positive reinforcement to help them gain confidence and motivation to keep cooking.

Cooking provides an opportunity to explore diverse cuisines and cultures from around the world. Preparing dishes from various cultural traditions can help children learn about new ingredients, flavors, and cooking techniques. Encourage them to ask questions, discover new foods, and appreciate the variety of global cuisine.

Cooking together as a family promotes bonding, laughter, and shared experiences. Capture these memories by taking photos, keeping a cooking journal, or starting a family recipe book with your children's favorite dishes. Use cooking to create lasting memories and strengthen family bonds.

Dental Health Tips for Parents

As parents, we understand that our children's dental health is an important part of their overall well-being. Developing good oral hygiene habits at a young age can pave the way for a lifetime of healthy teeth and gums. In addition to regular dental check-ups and brushing routines, parents can follow a variety of other tips and advice to help their children's dental health. Let's look at some key strategies for promoting good oral hygiene and preventing dental problems in children.

It's never too early to start caring for your child's oral health. When your child's first tooth appears, usually around six months old, start gently cleaning it with a soft, damp cloth or an infant toothbrush. This helps to eliminate bacteria and prevent decay from occurring.

Establish a daily routine for dental care, such as brushing twice and flossing once. Brushing your teeth should be a fun and enjoyable activity. Use colorful toothbrushes, flavored toothpaste, and sing songs or play games while brushing. Supervise young children to ensure they brush correctly and use the appropriate amount of toothpaste.

Select the Right Tools:

Choose age-appropriate toothbrushes and toothpaste for your child. Use a toothbrush with a small, soft bristle that is appropriate for infants and toddlers. Use a pea-sized amount of fluoride toothpaste for children aged 3 and up, and teach them to spit it out rather than swallow it. Encourage older children to clean the space between their teeth with dental floss or interdental brushes.

Monitor Diet and Nutrition:

Pay attention to your child's diet, and limit sugary snacks and beverages that can lead to tooth decay. Encourage healthy eating habits by serving a well-balanced diet rich in fruits, vegetables, whole grains, and lean proteins. Offer water or milk as the primary beverages, and limit consumption of sugary drinks like sodas and fruit juice.

Encourage water consumption as it benefits both overall health and dental health. Encourage your child to drink water all day, particularly after meals and snacks. Water helps to remove food particles and bacteria from the mouth, lowering the risk of cavities and promoting good oral hygiene.

Limit Sugary Treats: Even if you enjoy sweets occasionally, it's important to limit your intake, especially between meals. Sticky candies, sugary snacks, and carbonated beverages can all contribute to tooth decay if consumed in excess. Encourage healthier snacks like fresh fruits, vegetables, cheese, and yogurt.

Schedule regular dental checkups:

Regular dental check-ups are essential for monitoring your child's oral health and addressing any issues that arise early on. Schedule routine dental appointments for your child every six months, or as advised by their dentist. During these visits, the dentist can perform professional cleanings, check for cavities or other dental issues, and advise on proper oral hygiene practices.

To set a good example for your child, practice good oral hygiene yourself. Allow your child to see you brushing and flossing your teeth on a regular basis, emphasizing the importance of maintaining good oral health. When children see their parents consistently practicing healthy habits, they are more likely to follow suit.

Address Dental Anxiety: Some children may have dental anxiety or fear of going to the dentist. Talking with them about what to expect during dental appointments, selecting a child-friendly dentist, and providing reassurance and support throughout the process can all help to alleviate their fears. Encourage open communication and respond to any concerns they may have.

Stay up-to-date on pediatric dentistry trends and recommendations. Keep up with important topics like fluoride use, sealants, orthodontic treatment, and emergency dental care. Learn about common dental issues in children and how to recognize potential problems.

CONCLUSION

Additional Resources

In addition to the Dental Health Cookbook for Kids, there are numerous resources available to help children's dental health and promote healthy eating habits. These resources provide valuable information, tips, and activities to help children learn about oral hygiene and healthy food choices. Here are some additional resources to supplement the dental health cookbook for children:

Children's Books: There are numerous engaging and educational children's books available that discuss dental health and nutrition. These books frequently use colorful illustrations, fun characters, and interactive activities to teach children the value of brushing, flossing, and eating nutritious foods. Popular titles include Dr. Seuss' "The Tooth Book,"

Alicia Padron's "Brush, Brush, Brush!", and Stan and Jan Berenstain's "The Berenstain Bears Visit the Dentist."

Online Resources: The internet contains a wealth of information for parents and children interested in dental health and nutrition. Websites like the American Dental Association (ADA) and the Academy of Nutrition and Dietetics provide articles, videos, and interactive games to teach children about oral hygiene and healthy eating. These online resources provide useful information in a fun and user-friendly format.

Mobile Apps: There are several mobile apps available to help children learn about dental health and make healthy eating choices. These apps frequently include games, quizzes, and interactive tools to help kids learn about oral hygiene, nutrition, and the value of a healthy diet. Some popular dental health apps for kids are "Toothsavers Brushing Game" and "My Food Detective."

Educational videos can be an effective way to teach children about dental health and nutrition while keeping them entertained and engaged. YouTube, for example, has a large library of videos featuring dental professionals, nutritionists, and animated characters talking about brushing techniques, cavity prevention, and healthy eating habits. Parents can watch age-appropriate videos with their children to reinforce key concepts covered in the dental health cookbook.

Community Events: Many communities organize dental health and nutrition workshops for children and families. These events could include free dental screenings, interactive activities, cooking demonstrations, and educational presentations by dental professionals and nutrition experts. Parents can use local community calendars and websites to find upcoming events in their area and benefit from these valuable resources.

www.ingramcontent.com/pod-product-compliance
Lightning Source LLC
Chambersburg PA
CBHW070953250726
48663CB00002B/209